AF295010

Publisher: BoD · Books on Demand GmbH,
In de Tarpen 42, 22848 Norderstedt, bod@bod.de
Print: Libri Plureos GmbH, Friedensallee 273,
22763 Hamburg
ISBN: 978-3-7693-1935-4

Nikola Zora

Strange
little
poems

Jump

I'm going to fly high in the sky.
Nobody else is there
and I will fall to the ground.
The sound won't be pretty
and the city won't notice
that I'm gone.
They will say it was wrong
but for me, it was right.
This night I will fall
and never come back.
People will say it was caused
by my lack of understanding for the world.
Was it?
Maybe,
or so I let them think.

Please don't worry

You're worried about me?
Please don't say that.
The key to my death
is being hated by everyone.
Just for fun,
I tell them all that I want to die.
But you give me hope
and make me sigh in relieve
when I hold your hand
            after a panic attack.

You give me back my will to live.
But you're too good
            for someone like me.
So please
open your eyes and see,
that I'm no good for you.

The jester

I'm a jester,
a creator of fun and laughter.
The sun rises when my audience laughs
and it goes down when I show my wrath
to the one I trust the most.

I lost them in a minute
but my show doesn't have "finite".
I hate this meaningless feeling so much.
Now I must laugh to cover up my pain.
I am so low right now
but I must keep the show on
for everyone to see.

To fool them
I play a me with no pain whatsoever.
"You shall dance
          for their entertainment until
you drop dead from exhaustion!"

The jester did as he was told.
So he played and played until he stopped
and dropped right in the middle

of the stage.

They fell into a rage because of him.
One limb of his was broken,
another bruised, another one
		was full of blood.
The mud they threw was full of shame,
			embarassment
and too much hate as to bear it.

The clown became a disappointment
but still had to wear his costume,
so as to say it was funny
and throw a bunny to his audience
that will never stop watching.

It is forbidden

I'm hurting me
and it stays hidden.
But the thing I do it is forbidden.
I'm still doing it
because I'm worse than shit.
Others think so too,
they kick me with their shoe
and say I should just die.
I lie to my friends.
Say I'm good and fine
because that's the line they want to hear.
I'm so near to death
so I give up.

Error

An Error that's what I am.
I should disappear,
yet I'm still here.
Why won't you let me die?

As a little kid I wanted to fly,
but now I know what I am.

Useless, with no purpose whatsoever.
A feather that fell before my feet.
No angel possesses these,
the devil does.
Don't make a big fuss about it.
I will be with him soon,
just after noon
this Error will be corrected.

Flowers

A pair of flowers
drifting through the wind.
A fair decision
of picking them up.
A share of love
with the person they care for.
A private treasure
only for them.
A bit of love, shared,
only with you.
A confession
that I like you.

Blood does satisfiy

Love and hate
is not what it is expected to be.
Feelings are mixed
but on twenty-sixth of November
I will surrender to death.

How will I do it?
I'm not sure.
In my head there is a war
between the pills the doctor gave me
or the knife I use to cut,
with my luck I decide for the first,
or the second?

Because my thirst for blood
is not satisfied.
It is okay tho,
I will be dead soon anyways.

Black out

It was all red,
it looked so bad
but didn't hurt.
My shirt was all bloody
and it came out of my mouth.
Suddenly my south,
to the ground.
I didn't even make a sound, I think.
It was red everywhere,
no matter where I looked
It was like I booked a trip
      to the land of the dead
where I didn't want to go yet.

I was dizzy and then it was all black,
after my lack of consciousness
it was all white.
"The hospital"
I thought
then passed out again.

She seeks vengeance

But then I saw her
in this gloomy moonlight.
The eyes bloodier
than the red moon at night.

Before she fastly turned around
I could already admire
her black hair,
that was even more enchanting
than any spell ever cast.

She came into my sight
and I saw the delicate frame
of a woman like goddess,
her body indulged
in an endless ocean-blue dress
that seemed even brighter
than the day
yet even darker
than the night.

She looks less than a goddess,
more like she used

to be gods favourite
but is now a fallen angel instead.

Her beautiful appearance
burns itself into your eyes
like the hellish flames
that she rules over.

Even she was nice once
but her trust was broken
therefore her token
to heavens was shattered.

She chose the path of revenge
and became someone
whom everyone will remember forever.
Even more beautiful than a goddess
yet discarded by god himself.

We call her:
The Devil

Why

Why?
Thats all that's on my mind.
Why can't I wind back time?
Why did you leave me here to rot?
Why did you neglect me
            such an awful lot?

Was I not good enough for you?
Or were you there too when it happened?
I know you were,
why wouldn't you be?
I was drowning in the sea,
you stood there.

I remember now
the very moment now
when you pushed, hoping I'd die.
You were acting all shy
            in front of the others
then left me to die –
that covers the story pretty much.

I hate you,
I almost always did.
I touched the candle
you lit on fire.
You laughed as I was set ablaze.
In that case I'll end you first,
you cursed and wicked
fake "Best friend".

No Humanity

The voices in my head begin to whisper,
and my feet start to blister
as I wander around inside my own mind.
I need to find an answer
as to why I am like this.
I miss my humanity,
why can't I be normal?
I made a formal request to death
to release me from this pain.
I wanted to gain humanity
but I guess there's no hope
       for someone like me.
The only thing I wished for
was to see how people would treat me,
if they saw me as a person.

The Spellbook

She betrayed me
so I look for a way to hurt her
in this old, old book.

I found this spell that I want to cast
in my last moments,
I recite the curse:

Dark night in the forest at fall
I never had these feelings at all.
The gods will make it look fair,
she was never even there.
Bloody rabit, sacred cow
I want her to be miserable right now.

Now that all of this is set:
I wish I hadn't even met her yet.
I'm tired now
so I will go,
did it work?
That will show itself.

Die tote Schwalbe

Die Schwalbe singt
doch ob sie klingt
    können nur die Toten sagen.
Die Schwalbe führt sie übers Meer,
die Berge und das Heer
    der feindlich gesinnten Leute.
Die euch ansehen wie ihre Beute,
die sie töten
und unwissend zur Schwalbe schicken.

Die Strafe der Götter

Der Gott wird zum Schafott gebracht
doch er schreit
zu den Göttern dort reiht:
"Nur der Körper wird vergehen
die Seele bleibt für immer!"
Doch nun rollt sein Kopf
und die Götter scholten:
"Die Strafe Himmels
        hat dich empfangen!
Doch du lebst immer noch!"
"Poch, Poch machte das Herz zuletzt."
sagte der Gott zuletzt.

Numb

There's a killer in my mirror
where I would like to hide,
where I would like to cry or just be sad.
There's a murder on my mind
where I would like to hurt
or just kill me.

My shirt is full of blood,
my arms are full of scars,
my mind is full of thoughts
and it's tearing me apart.
I don't trust my friends
if I have some.

But it doesn't bother me
because I feel so numb.

Mein dummes Leben

Am Abhang ich stehe,
ich gehe doch ich stehe
was it es denn nun?
Was ist dieses "denn" und "nun"?
Ach es sind nur Worte
      die sich kreuseln
und auch scheuseln
      in meinem Kopf herum.
Ach es ist so dumm dass ich lebe
und meinen Körper pflege
wenn ich tot sein kann.
Also dann, auf ein Wiedersehen
vielleicht,
doch ich hoffe ja nicht ich werde
dies überstehen
sogleich.

Failure

He whined and ended up
              comitting a crime
"Pity yourself and life becomes
              an endless nightmare",
Dazai once said.
I'm gonna go ahead
and kill myself now,
I'm gonna bow to death
              and let him take me.
He will lead me
to the end of the light.
It's not heaven
nor is it hell.
That's where I will go
and stay for eternity.
I'm a failure for nothing great
my death comes late,
but I hope, this once
I will serve a purpose.

"No longer Human"

I can no longer be called "human",
but what does that matter to me?
I try to drown myself in the sea,
but fail over and over again.
So I began to try more,
a rope and a knife.
In my eyes
my life has no value.
I don't know how others see this.
They say: "You're important to me!"
But I dismiss it as an insult
directed to my mind.
"You must find a reason to live!"
someone said to me and I replied:
"Do you really think there is any value,
to this thing we call living?"

Appearently I
led him to suicide
one week later.
They say its my fault
but I bet its theirs.

"No longer Human,
thats what you are!" they said.
"I didn't drive him mad!"
After support there is betrayal,
that's how it's always been for me.
So let me drown in this sea,
for the purpose of never experiencing
that again.

They thought wrong

There was once a girl
whom everyone loved,
but their fake feelings were shoved aside
everytime she made a mistake.

Even when someone only got a headache,
it was only her to blame.
They all said "Be ashamed of yourself!"
She put up with everything
until the she finally broke
and she snapped and said:
"I wish you could just
            open your eyes and see
that the girl I'm pretending to be
            isn't me!"
With these words she went away,
and they still say she'll return someday.

I don't think so,
please believe me instead, okay?
Because I was once such a girl
but I never returned.

Please tell me

I wanna fall asleep
to the sound of your voice.
I wanna hear you speak
through the night.
I wanna hear the words
spreading from your mouth.
I want to listen to your sounds
from north, east, west and south.
No matter what you want to tell me
I will listen.
And I'll savour every word
because when you're gone
I dont know how much I'll miss them.

Re-new the cuts

Selfharm –
What does that even exactly mean?
I've tried getting clean numerous times
but it was always the voice in my head
that chimes in and says "Do it!"
My desire to bleed lit up
            after that everytime
and it just won't disappear.

I start tearing up,
What is wrong with me?
Just let me flee from this reality!
Even my favourite music
with the volume at its highest
            isn't working.
Should I just give in and start cutting?
In the past I started shutting
            myself in my room
whenever things got too bad
but people will get suspicious
            if I do that now.
I'll just need to wear long sleeves
and play it cool.

I am such a fool
to keep on staying here
but don't worry,
I'll be paying for it tonight.
There is my razor blade
what perfect timing,
my scars were just starting to fade.
It doesn't even hurt
there's just so much blood.
All these thoughts flood my mind
          right now
but I pay them no mind.
How kind of you bandages
          to put up with my blood
all these cuts will be re-newed
          tomorrow.

Don't be like me

As I was walking down the street
a little girl tagged at my sleeve and said
"I know we just we met but
        oh beautiful lady
will having a pretty face
        make it better?"
"In no case will that improve
        things like we want"
I answered, the girl's front seemed happy
but I knew what was really going on.

My face saddened
as I saw how she was putting on a con
for people
I couldn't help but hug her
I lured into this faint moment
        of happiness
and I could already see her eyes
starting to sparkle with tears.
All her fears disappeared
        within that second
she knew she wanted to cry

because of her lack
and she almost gave in.

She could feel how thin
        the beautiful lady was
only skin and bones.
She was starving herself
while everyone around only looked
        at their phones.
"Don't become like me kid,"
she said with a sad smile
before walking away.
She fit right in
even though no one as as pretty as her.
The little girl thought, wiping her tears
but not smiling through the pain
as she took the lady's words to heart.

Die Legende des Werwolfs

Der Schnee glänzt weiß
gerufen aus dem Mondeskreis
so sagt es die Legende.
Der Werwolf zieht
ohne jede Spur
seine Tour.
An den Körper
haben die Menschen das Silber geschnallt.
DOCH HALT!
Frisst er Menschen oder nicht?
Was besagt denn die Geschicht?
Doch die Wahrheit ist
er löscht nur jedes Licht.

I want to live

Right now I'm just sitting here
letting my fear consume.
I thought I went insane due to
this excruciating pain,
but now I only feel so hollow.
All this time I followed my brain
but in the end, what did I gain?
What's the use to strain myself like this?
Is it truly worth it?
My life feels like shit
and no matter what I change
I always end up in range of my knife.
Why do I even bother with this life?
But at my core
I want to live
I don't care how stiff or ugly
          it's gonna get.
I wanna live.

Mad Freedom

How stupid must someone be
to be as dumb as me?
I have all this useless hope
I don't want to say I'm fine
but I must.

This line will keep them from worrying
Why can't they all just hate me?
Then I would be free
to die whenever without them sad.
All of this is driving me mad
All this pressure is simply too much
I can only clutch my fists and teeth
while going through this hell.
I don't know if I tripped
but I fell from a roof.

Somehow this terrible pain soothes me
and is comforting.
It tells me that all this is over
I will be gone.

I feel like a con-man
whose show has come to an end
I'm sorry my friend
But please don't miss me
as I am finally free.

Der Rausch des Alltags

Im Rausch der Drogen rieche ich
den Pausch des Weins
doch es ist nur der Plausch der Blumen.
Die Bäume reden und die Blätter schweben
auf nach Schweden in den Norden
zu den Horden von Tod und Leben
und ich bin an den Zweigen der Reben
zwischen Hölle und Himmel.
Bin ich lebendig?
Bin ich tot?
Das ist mir egal auf dieser Reise, paschal.
Ich wache auf und bin wieder im Lauf
des langweiligen Alltags.

Eine tödliche Melodie

Heute bin ich nicht unterwegs
und doch bin ich es stets
zur Schule, zum Park,
ich bestell mir nun einfach einen Sarg
denn ich werd's nicht mehr lange machen.
Was tu ich denn für Sachen?
In meinem Kopf da ist mein Leck
um mich zu töten.
Wenn du willst kannst du es löten
Doch das wird nichts bringen
denn ich höre den Tod schon singen
der kommt um mich zu holen.

Blutiger Boden

Glück, werde ich es jemals finden?
Immer wenn es zum greifen nah ist
scheint es zu verschwinden.
An diese Welt bindet mich
       höchstens meine Freunde.
Sollte ich es einfach tun?
Nun, das Messer ist in meiner Hand
Oh Gott, ich sehe die roten Gewässer
       auf dem Boden schon.
Das ganze Blut ist mein Lohn
für diese schrecklichen vier Jahre.
Es ist es wert, ich kehre
       diesem Leben den Rücken
und gehe über die Grenze hinüber
in den Tod.

Clown no longer

I feel like a clown
Only my parents frown everytime I do
          something wrong.
Of course they don't laugh,
I mean what's so funny about
          a grave mistake such as I?

But of course I die inside while still
          smiling with my outer shell.

"You're doing everything wrong!"
"I know."

I'm so tired of putting on a show
I'm so sorry for this huge blow
          Mom and Dad
You expected me to be perfect but
          I went mad under this pressure.

I can't be your high-achieving kid
I don't fit the things
          you want to see in me.

And so I flee,

I ran far, far away
because I didn't want to obey you
        anymore.

I'm happier now then I've ever been
        with you
"I don't even regognize who you are
        anymore!"
That's because you never knew me,
        no you never even tried.

That is exactly why I cried
        myself to sleep every night.
I still fight with my emotions
        but at least
I don't think I'm the problem anymore.

A starless night

As I lie here I look up at the sky
      wanting to see stars
But the clouds up there are blocking
      my view
While seeing this, I think of you
Who is as numb as the display
      before my eyes.

I think of all the lies you've told
Were they just for you?
Or did someone wish for you to survive
      on this cold night?
It can't be that you loved them,
      you were as numb as one can be
Is that why you flee from this life?

To live wasn't your choice
It is as though you always already were
      on a cliff
just waiting to jump off.

I cough up blood again
Why would I live when you are gone?

That's why I took the poison
I know you wouldn't want me to fawn
            over your death like this
Yet I can't help but think of you
On a numb night like this.

Dried Tears

I can't cry anymore
I've done it so much
That I'm completely dry now.

I'm unable to smile as well.
My outer shell just can't pretend
no more.

This whole time my very core
couldn't take it.
But no matter what,
I always endured their shit
with a sweet grin on my lips.
But the more I acted,
the more scars filled my hips.
Just more and more, never enough.

The blood on my arms is as dry
            as the tears
that used to roll down my face.
I always cut in this place,
seeing the water rinse my wounds
feels so numb.

This was a dumb idea,
I never should have hid it
and just got help.

My Art

It's quite common
for artists to draw on their skin.
I myself drew with a thin needle
but now a razor blade.
My art is just starting to fade.
"So draw deeper" says my brain.
That faint suggestion is enough
to encourage me to draw even more.
This art is precious
I need it for coping.
Drawing like this always helps me
not to draw on my wrists.
My fists are clenched
as I endure the pain
from my art when someone grabs me.
I want to stab my art
and my heart shatters at that thought.

Contents